P.43 (Price increase)

Ⓔ 14.96 Correction

Ⓟ 6.95

Age 90 up

B/4 of
Ⓤ
$12.95

THE USBORNE GEOGRAPHY QUIZBOOK

Marit Claridge and Paul Dowswell

Edited by Judy Tatchell

Designed by Ruth Russell

Illustrated by Chris Lyon

Additional design and illustration by
Richard Johnson and Rachel Lockwood

Consultant: John Brennan

Contents

About this book

The surface of the Earth is immensely varied. This book looks at our planet, from mountains to rainforests, oceans to cities. It explains how the planet provides its inhabitants with air, water and food, and shows why we need to protect the Earth from the growing threat of pollution.

How to do the quizzes

Throughout the book there are quiz questions to answer as you go along, printed in italic type, *like this*. Some of the questions rely on your general knowledge, others have clues elsewhere on the page. Keep a note of your answers and check them against the answers on page 28-31.

The Megaquiz

On pages 26-27 is the Megaquiz – a set of ten quick quizzes to test you on your general knowledge and what you have read about in the book.

The Earth in space

Planet Earth is a huge ball of rock which spins in space. Earth is one of the smallest of nine planets which circle around a central star, called the Sun. A group of planets circling around a star is called a solar system.

What is a star?

A star is a burning ball of gas which gives off heat and light. The Sun is a star. It is part of a group of millions of stars, called a galaxy. There are about 200,000 million stars in our galaxy which is called the Milky Way. Many stars are bigger than the Sun.

1. A solar system is made up of a star and: a) a Sun; b) a galaxy; c) planets.

The Milky Way

Sun

Mercury

Venus

Moon

Earth

Mars

The farthest that anyone has ever traveled is to the Moon. The first men landed on the Moon on July 20, 1969.

4. Is the Moon a star?

5. The first man on the moon was: a) Christopher Columbus; b) Neil Armstrong; c) Flash Gordon.

6. Which is the coldest planet?

Jupiter

One of Jupiter's 12 moons. A moon circles around a planet, not around the Sun.

Asteroids – rocks circling the Sun.

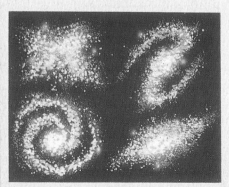

Your address in space would look like this:

Name
House
Street
Town
Country
The Earth
The Solar System
The Milky Way
The Universe

7. Which planet is named after the Roman goddess of love?

8. Which is bigger, a solar system or the Milky Way?

9. Unscramble these words to find the names of two planets: I STAR JUMPER.

Uranus

What is the Universe?

Our galaxy, the Milky Way, is part of a group of about thirty galaxies. Beyond this there may be more than 200,000 million other galaxies. Together they make up the Universe. No one knows how big the Universe is.

2. Is the Earth the center of the Universe?

3. Distances between stars are measured in: a) light years; b) string; c) gallons.

Four galaxies in the Universe.

Why does it get dark at night?

The Earth spins around all the time. It takes about 24 hours to spin around once. As it spins, some parts of it face away from the Sun and are in shadow (night time) and some parts have sunlight (daytime).

In the picture, follow the red dot in Africa from night to day.

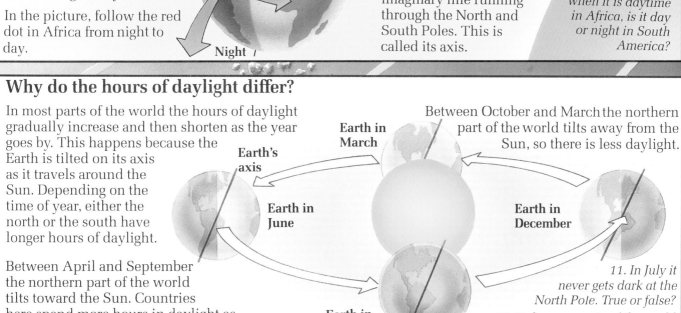

Earth's axis

Day

Night

Sun

The Earth spins on an imaginary line running through the North and South Poles. This is called its axis.

10. In the picture, when it is daytime in Africa, is it day or night in South America?

Why do the hours of daylight differ?

In most parts of the world the hours of daylight gradually increase and then shorten as the year goes by. This happens because the Earth is tilted on its axis as it travels around the Sun. Depending on the time of year, either the north or the south have longer hours of daylight.

Between April and September the northern part of the world tilts toward the Sun. Countries here spend more hours in daylight as the Earth goes through its 24 hour spin.

Between October and March the northern part of the world tilts away from the Sun, so there is less daylight.

Earth in March

Earth's axis

Earth in June

Earth in December

Earth in September

11. In July it never gets dark at the North Pole. True or false?

12. Only some parts of the world have 24 hours in a day. True or false?

Saturn

Saturn's rings – these are made of millions of ice-covered rocks.

One of Saturn's moons.

Did you know?

The Earth circles the Sun at a speed of 29.8km (18.5 miles) per second. It takes 365¼ days to make one complete circle around the Sun.

We use the 365 days to measure one year. Every fourth year the extra quarters are added together to make a year with 366 days, which is called a leap year.

13. Do all planets have moons?

14. Is there life on Neptune?

Neptune

15. Is a New Moon visible?

Pluto

Why does the Moon change shape?

The half of the Moon facing the Sun is always lit up. As the Moon goes around Earth, you see different parts of this half. The Moon takes about a month to go around the Earth.

The bottom part of the picture shows the Moon in five positions which it passes through on its way around Earth. The pink band shows what the Moon looks like from Earth.

Full Moon	Gibbous Moon	Quarter Moon	Crescent Moon	New Moon	Moon as seen from Earth.

Moon

Earth

Sunlight. The Moon is always lit by the Sun but what you can see of it, shown in the pink band above, changes.

3

The surface of the Earth

If you could look at the Earth from space, you would see a brownish-green blue and white planet, half hidden in swirling clouds. The blue oceans make up 71% of the surface of the Earth. The brownish-green areas are the land, which is in seven main blocks, called continents.

   People live on about a third of the land on Earth. Some parts are crowded. Others, such as deserts, are nearly empty.

1. Seen from space, what color would the Arctic and Antarctic be?

2. Which is the largest continent?

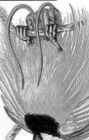

The areas around the North and South Poles are frozen all the time. The North Pole is in the middle of the Arctic Ocean.

3. Do people live at the North Pole?

Mountains cover nearly a quarter of the land on Earth. They are cold places and few people live there.

4. Mountains make good farmland. True or false?

Arctic Ocean

5. In which continent are the Himalayas?

Europe

Asia

North America

Pacific Ocean

The Pacific Ocean is the largest ocean. It covers nearly one third of the surface of the Earth.

Atlantic Ocean

Africa

Indian Ocean

Australia

The South Pole is in the continent of Antarctica.

6. Are there more people or penguins in Antarctica?

South America

There are volcanoes, valleys, plains and mountains on the ocean floor, just as there are on land.

Antarctic Ocean

Antarctica

Deserts have almost no water. The Sahara is the largest desert in the world.

7. The Sahara covers almost one third of Africa. True or false?

Most people live on flat land in places that are neither too hot nor too cold. Many people live along rivers where there is rich farmland.

8. The River Nile flows through: a) Ecuador; b) Egypt; c) England.

Very few people live in the hot, wet rainforests around the middle of the Earth.

9. Brazil has the largest rainforest. True or false?

4

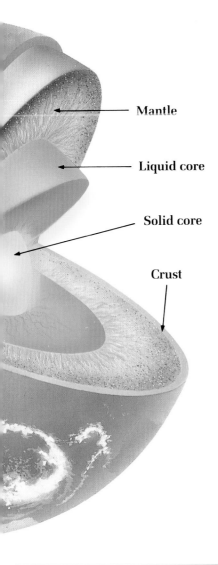

Mantle

Liquid core

Solid core

Crust

Is the Earth solid?

The Earth is made up of layers. The continents and oceans are part of an outer layer of solid rock called the crust. This rests on hot, toffee-like rock called the mantle.

The center of the Earth, the core, is made of very hot, heavy rock. Scientists think that the core is liquid on the outside and solid in the middle.

Do the continents move?

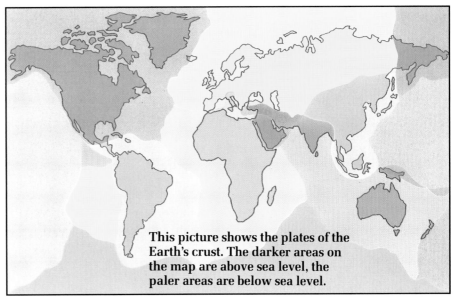

This picture shows the plates of the Earth's crust. The darker areas on the map are above sea level, the paler areas are below sea level.

The continents are part of the Earth's crust which is made up of several huge pieces, like a big jigsaw puzzle. These pieces, or plates, are shown on the map. The mantle underneath the crust is heated by the liquid rocks around the Earth's core. This sets up currents in the mantle, in the same way that boiling water swirls around in a saucepan. These currents move some of the plates together while other plates move apart. The main mountain ranges, volcanoes and earthquake zones all run along the edges of the plates.

10. Is it hotter at the center of the Earth or in the Sahara desert?

11. Africa was once joined to America. True or false?

Did you know?

The Earth's crust is about 64km (40 miles) thick. If the Earth was the size of a soccer ball, the crust would be the thickness of a postage stamp.

What happens when the Earth's crust moves?

When plates move together, the crust is slowly pushed up into folds. These are mountains. The highest mountains in the world, the Himalayas, were formed when India bumped into Asia.

12. The lowest places on Earth are at the bottom of: a) the sea; b) lakes; c) mineshafts.

Pressure builds up as plates push or slide against each other. If the pressure becomes too great the rocks suddenly snap and move, shaking the ground. This is called an earthquake.

13. Which of these cities is famous for its earthquakes: a) Paris; b) San Francisco; c) Sydney?

Volcanoes occur along the edges of plates as these are the weakest spots in the Earth's crust. The hot, liquid rock under the crust forces its way through the surface as a volcano.

14. Can volcanoes erupt under the sea?

15. What is the name of the world's highest mountain?

Volcano

Plates pressing together. ⟶

Folds of rock

Mapping the world

A map is a picture of any part of the Earth. A map can be of a very small area, such as a museum, or of a whole country, a continent or the whole world.

Maps can show different things, such as roads or what sort of food is grown in an area. They help you to find out where places are on the Earth and how to get there.

How are flat maps made of the Earth?

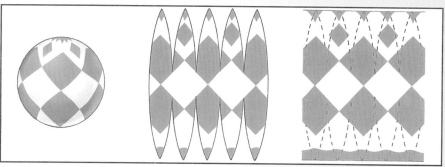

It is difficult to draw a flat map of the Earth because the Earth is ball-shaped. The picture above shows how a map-maker might draw a map of a ball. The ball is divided into segments which are then spread out flat. Parts of the ball have to be stretched on the map to fill the gaps between the segments.

In the same way, map-makers have to change the shape of countries slightly to make flat maps of the Earth. There are several ways of stretching out a ball-shape to fit on a flat surface. These are called projections. The maps above show how two different projections make

Australia appear to be two different shapes.

1. Which is more accurate, a globe or a flat map?

2. Which continent is missing from this list: Australia, Europe, Africa, North America, Antarctica, South America?

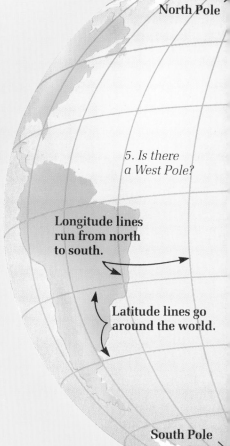

5. Is there a West Pole?

Longitude lines run from north to south.

Latitude lines go around the world.

North Pole

South Pole

Which way up?

The four main directions used on maps are north, south, east and west.

North is the direction towards the North Pole from anywhere on Earth. South is the direction towards the South Pole. When you face north, the direction to your left is west and to your right is east. North is normally at the top of a map.

6. What is the direction half way between north and east?

What is a political map?

A political map shows how the Earth is divided up into countries. A country is an area which is usually run by its own government. This political map shows the countries in South America.

3. Would you use a political map to find a country's borders, or to find where mountains are?

4. How many countries are there in South America?

How do you find North?

You can use a compass to find out which way you are facing. The needle of a compass always points north.

Turn the compass until the needle points to letter N. You can then see which way is west, east or south.

7. Which direction is at the bottom of most maps?

Longitude 0° runs through Greenwich in England.

Latitude 0° is called the Equator. It is half way between the North and South Poles.

8. Can space travelers see latitude and longitude lines on the Earth?

9. Greenwich is in: a) Madrid; b) Paris; c) London.

Why are there lines on a map?

Lines are drawn on maps to divide them into sections. The lines help you to find places on a map. On continental and world maps, the distances between the lines are measured in degrees (°).

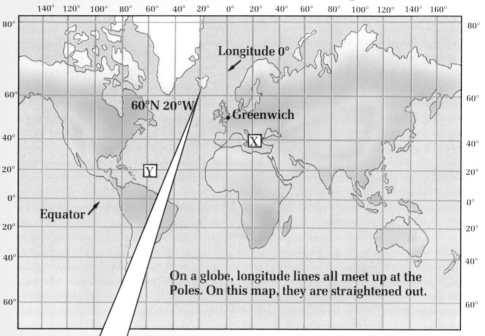

Longitude 0°

60°N 20°W

Greenwich

X

Y

Equator

On a globe, longitude lines all meet up at the Poles. On this map, they are straightened out.

Imagine two ships colliding at sea. They radio for help and tell the rescue services that their position is 60°N and 20°W. This means 60° north of the Equator and 20° west of longitude 0° (the north-south line running through Greenwich). The rescue service can pinpoint their position at once and direct any nearby ship to their aid.

10. Are the ships nearer North America or Europe?

11. If a volcano erupted at point X on the map, what would its position be?

12. If a hurricane was approaching Central America from point Y, what would its position be?

Did you know?

You can use the stars to find your direction. In the northern half of the world (called the northern hemisphere), look for a group of stars called Ursa Major*. A line through the end of Ursa Major points to the North Star. This is directly above the North Pole.

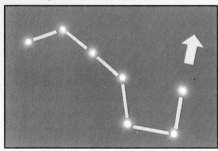

In the southern hemisphere, look for the Southern Cross to find which way is south.

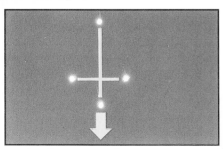

*Also known as the Big Dipper.

What is a physical map?

A physical map shows the Earth's natural features – such as rivers, mountains and valleys. Lines on some maps, called contour lines, indicate the height of the land in regular intervals. The closer together these lines are, the steeper the slope. This map shows the coastline at the bottom of the page.

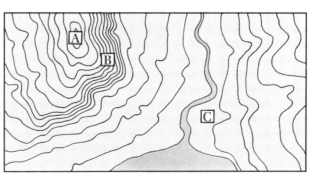

A

B

C

13. Is there flat land on the map at A, B or C?

14. Is it very steep at A, B or C?

15. Is A, B or C at the top of a hill?

The Earth's atmosphere

The Earth is wrapped in a layer of air, called the atmosphere. The air acts like a blanket around the Earth. During the day it protects the Earth from the Sun's harmful rays. At night it stops heat from leaving the Earth.

Air is a mixture of gases. The main gas is nitrogen. Most of the rest, about 20% of air, is oxygen.

1. Which gas do you need to breathe in order to stay alive?

How high is the sky?

The Earth's atmosphere is about 32km (20 miles) thick. Beyond this is space and the other planets and stars in the Universe. The picture below shows what happens at different levels of the atmosphere.

32km (20 miles) — Scientists send research balloons up to 30km (18 miles) high.

18km (11 miles) — There may be clouds in the sky up to here.

16km (10 miles) — The weather affects the atmosphere up to about this level.

15km (9.3 miles) — Jets cruise at about this level.

8.8km (5.5 miles) — Mount Everest

2. Are jets affected by storms?

3. At 0km (0 miles) it is: a) ground level; b) sea level; c) sky level.

Did you know?

Although you cannot feel the air around you, it does have a weight. Altogether the air in the Earth's atmosphere weighs about 5,500 million tons. The weight of air is called air pressure.

4. Air pressure is less at the top of a mountain than at sea level. True or false?

What causes the wind?

The air around the Earth is always moving. You feel this moving air as wind.

At the Equator the land heats the air. Warm air is lighter than cold air so it rises. Warm air rising makes an area of low air pressure. Cold air is pulled in from elsewhere to take the place of the warm air.

At the Poles, air presses down on the Earth and makes an area of high air pressure. The wind is caused by air moving from areas of high pressure to low pressure areas.

5. Is it hot or cold at the Equator?

6. Which of these tells which way the wind is blowing: a) weather vane; b) compass; c) barometer?

Cold air presses heavily on the surface of the Earth.

Warm air rises.

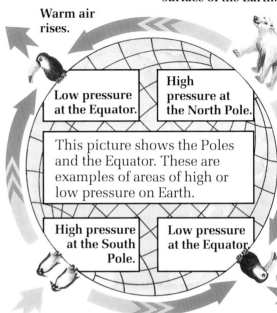

Low pressure at the Equator.

High pressure at the North Pole.

This picture shows the Poles and the Equator. These are examples of areas of high or low pressure on Earth.

High pressure at the South Pole.

Low pressure at the Equator.

Cold air, as wind, flows to take the place of rising warm air.

What are weather and climate?

Weather is sunshine, wind, rain, snow, etc. In some parts of the world, the weather is much the same day after day. In other places, the weather changes all the time.

A place's climate is the average amount of sunshine, wind and rainfall that it has, year after year.

7. It is warmer on a mountain top, which is nearer the Sun, than at sea level. True or false?

You see rainbows when sunlight shines through raindrops.

Snowflakes are made of tiny ice crystals. Each one is different.

8. Which has more changeable weather, the Sahara desert or Great Britain?

9. Are weather and climate the same thing?

What are clouds?

Clouds are patches of air which contain millions of tiny drops of water. Clouds have different shapes and are at different heights. Some are shown below.

Cirrus clouds are very high and are made of tiny ice crystals. They usually mean rain is coming.

Cirrocumulus clouds are a sign of unsettled weather.

Cumulonimbus clouds often bring thunderstorms with rain, snow or hail.

Cumulus clouds appear in sunny, summer skies.

Stratus cloud is a low blanket of cloud which often brings drizzle.

Fog is cloud at ground level.

10. Which are the highest clouds in the sky?

11. Smog is a mixture of smoke and: a) rain; b) smelly dog; c) fog.

What are thunder and lightning?

Lightning makes the air it goes through very hot. The air expands violently, like an explosion, and makes a clap of thunder. Below, you can see what causes lightning.

Inside cumulonimbus clouds, particles of water and ice move up and down in air currents.
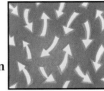

As the water and ice rub against each other, there is a build-up of static electricity.

The electricity builds up until there is a giant spark. You see this as a flash of lightning.

You can tell how far away a thunderstorm is by counting the time between the lightning and the first clap of thunder. The distance is about 2km (about a mile) for every five seconds.

12. If you hear thunder ten seconds after seeing lightning, how far away is the storm?

13. Are there more thunderstorms at the Equator or at the Poles?

What are hurricanes and tornadoes?

A hurricane is a violent storm with strong winds and rain. Areas of extremely low pressure build up over warm oceans. Warm, wet air spins into the middle of the low pressure area causing the strong winds. The warm air rises and the water vapor in it becomes clouds and heavy rain.

14. Hurricanes have eyes. True or false?

A tornado is like a very small hurricane. It is a whirling funnel of upward-spinning air. Winds in a tornado reach up to 500kmph (300mph). They suck up anything in their path, sometimes even people, animals and cars.

15. Tornadoes can pick up trains. True or false?

9

Rivers and rain

Plants and animals need water to stay alive. Your body is about 75% water. Without water, your body would not work.

Only 3% of the water on Earth is fresh water. The rest is salty. Two thirds of the Earth's fresh water is frozen in ice sheets and glaciers. The remaining third is in rivers, lakes and water underground.

1. Camels can survive without water for: a) 21; b) 7; c) 2 days.

Where does water come from?

There is always the same amount of water on Earth. It moves from place to place. When a puddle dries up, the water does not disappear. Tiny particles of water rise from the puddle. They become a gas called water vapor. This is called evaporation.

When water vapor rises into cooler air, it turns back into tiny water droplets and becomes clouds and rain. The movement of water from the land to the air and back to the land is called the water cycle.

Rainwater soaks into the soil and rocks. It slowly seeps into lakes and rivers.

Clouds form when air containing water vapor rises and cools.

Rainwater runs off slopes into lakes and rivers.

Plants absorb water from the ground. They release it back into the air through their leaves.

Water evaporates.

2. When washing dries, the water in it: a) disappears; b) becomes water vapor; c) becomes air.

3. What are clouds made of?

4. In big cities, each glass of water someone drinks has already been drunk by someone else. True or false?

5. Is there water vapor in your breath?

Where do rivers begin?

Rivers begin in hills and mountains as small streams. They carry rainwater from the land to the sea. A river gets bigger as it collects more and more water on its way.

6. Which of these rivers is the shortest: a) Thames; b) Nile; c) Amazon?

As the water flows downhill it sweeps away small pieces of rock. These rub at the bottom and sides of the stream and make it wider and deeper.

Rivers flood when there is more rain than usual on the land which drains into the river.

7. Some rivers flow uphill. True or false?

Did you know?

You need to drink about 1.7 litres (3 pints) of water a day. Where there is plenty of water, each person uses about 20 times as much as this a day, for washing, cooking, etc.

8. What happens to water at 0°C (32°F)?

9. You can live without water for: a) a day; b) four days; c) a month.

What is hydroelectricity?

The power in falling water can be used to make electricity, which is then called hydroelectricity. The water is trapped by a dam. It is then piped to a power station where it flows over big water wheels, called turbines. These turn generators which make electricity.

River water also has enormous power. It wears away rocks and shapes the land into hills and valleys.

10. Hydroelectric power stations are only found in flat areas. True or false?

11. What do hydroelectric, tidal and wave power have in common?

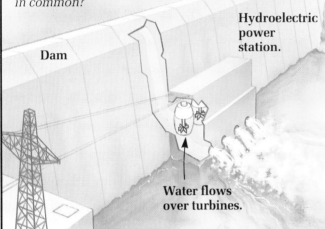

Dam

Hydroelectric power station.

Water flows over turbines.

How is a waterfall made?

When a river flows from hard to softer rock, the softer rock wears away more quickly and makes a small step. The water falls over the step on to the soft rock below, wearing it away even more. Gradually the step and the waterfall get bigger.

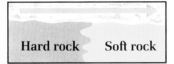

Hard rock **Soft rock**

Waterfall

The highest waterfall in the world is Angel Falls in Venezuela. The river drops 979m (3,214ft).

12. Which of these is not a famous waterfall: a) Niagara; b) Grand Canyon; c) Victoria?

What is water pollution?

Many towns and factories are built near rivers so that they can use the water. Sometimes towns and factories pour dirty water back into the rivers. The rivers become dirty, or "polluted". Pollution can make rivers smell and can kill water plants and animals. Polluted rivers drain into the sea and pollute the sea as well. (See pages 24-25 for more about pollution.)

13. Fish caught in polluted rivers can be poisonous. True or false?

Farmers spray chemicals on fields to make crops grow better. The chemicals may drain into streams and rivers and pollute them.

People sometimes dump garbage in rivers. As garbage rots, it uses up oxygen in the water. Fish may die due to lack of oxygen.

Some harmful cleaning chemicals in waste water from homes remain harmful even after treatment in a sewage treatment plant.

Garbage from towns is often buried in huge holes in the ground. Chemicals in garbage can drain through the ground into rivers.

What is a glacier?

Glaciers are rivers of ice. They occur in very cold areas and on high mountains. When snow falls here it crushes snow beneath it to ice. The snow and ice slide slowly down the mountain.

Glacier

14. Glaciers are found in: a) Mexico; b) Great Britain; c) Scandinavia.

U-shaped valley

Glaciers wear away the sides and bottoms of valleys. They leave behind deep U-shaped valleys.

15. Which flows faster, a river or a glacier?

Oceans and coasts

Nearly three quarters of the Earth's surface is covered by oceans. There are five oceans (see page 4) and they contain smaller areas called seas. The coast is where the land meets the sea.

The shape of the coasts is always changing. Waves pound at beaches and cliffs, slowly wearing them away. The sea also drops sand and mud in sheltered areas. This builds up and becomes new land.

1. Are all the oceans joined together?

2. Which of these is a sea, not an ocean: a) Atlantic; b) Pacific; c) Mediterranean; d) Indian?

Why is the sea salty?

Water dissolves salt in rocks on the ocean floor. On land, streams and rivers carry salt from rocks to the sea. Also, water evaporates from the sea leaving the salt behind.

River water does not taste salty because a river is continually filled with fresh water from rain or thawing snow. There is only a small amount of salt in it at any one time.

3. Can salt be collected from the sea?

4. There is gold in seawater. True or false?

How are cliffs formed?

Cliffs are formed where a hard band of rock meets the sea. Waves carrying small pebbles break against the rock just above sea level. They erode, or eat into it, and a small cliff is made. The sea continues to eat away at the rock and makes an overhang. In time the overhang breaks off, leaving a bigger cliff for the sea to beat against.

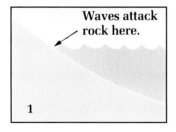
Waves attack rock here.
1

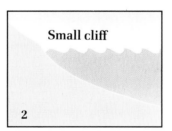
Small cliff
2

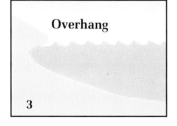
Overhang
3

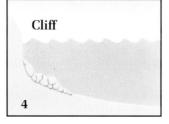
Cliff
4

5. Cliffs can form overnight. True or false?

6. Cliffs are only found on the coast. True or false?

How are beaches made?

Waves wash sand along the coast. When they reach a sheltered area they slow down, and drop the sand. In time, the sand builds up into beaches. Beaches are often found in sheltered bays.

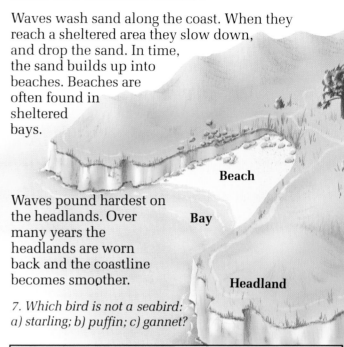
Beach

Bay

Headland

Waves pound hardest on the headlands. Over many years the headlands are worn back and the coastline becomes smoother.

7. Which bird is not a seabird: a) starling; b) puffin; c) gannet?

The sea sometimes drops sand in the shelter of a headland. This makes a ridge of sand, called a spit.

Headland

Bay

Spit

What is sand?

Sand is tiny particles of rock. It is washed into the sea by rivers and made when waves grind down rocky cliffs. Sand is also made from broken down shells, and coral which is washed ashore from nearby reefs. Few plants can grow in the sand on the beach, but many tiny creatures live in it.

8. Do you find sand dunes on beaches or on cliff tops?

Did you know?

The icebergs that float in the oceans of the far north and far south of the world come from glaciers (see page 11). Some glaciers flow down from mountains into the sea, and huge chunks of ice break off them and float away. Icebergs also break off from the thick sheet of ice that covers most of Antarctica. Frozen water does not contain salt, so all icebergs are made up of fresh water.

9. How much of an iceberg can you see above water: a) one half; b) one quarter; c) one eighth?

10. Which famous British cruise liner was sunk on its first voyage in 1912, by an iceberg in the Atlantic?

How do people use the sea?

The picture below shows how people use the oceans and coasts for energy, transportation food and pleasure. Careless use of the sea has damaged this environment, though. Look for the red boxes which describe some of the ways in which people have polluted the sea.

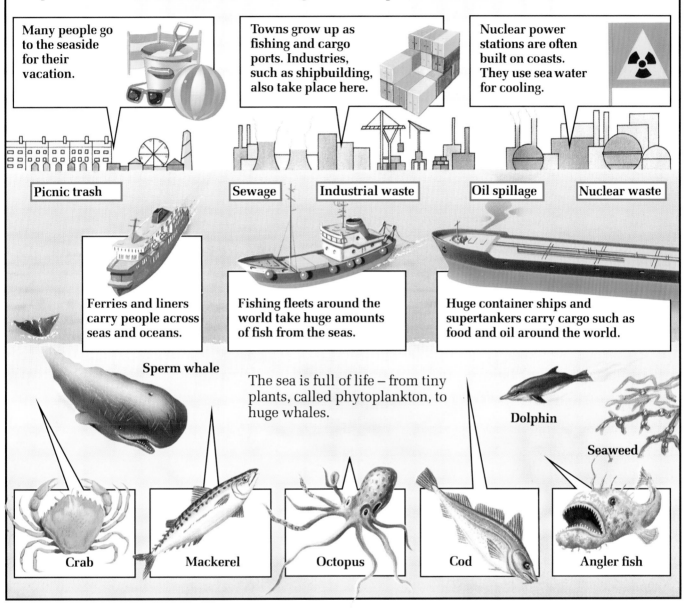

Many people go to the seaside for their vacation.

Towns grow up as fishing and cargo ports. Industries, such as shipbuilding, also take place here.

Nuclear power stations are often built on coasts. They use sea water for cooling.

Picnic trash

Sewage

Industrial waste

Oil spillage

Nuclear waste

Ferries and liners carry people across seas and oceans.

Fishing fleets around the world take huge amounts of fish from the seas.

Huge container ships and supertankers carry cargo such as food and oil around the world.

Sperm whale

The sea is full of life – from tiny plants, called phytoplankton, to huge whales.

Dolphin

Seaweed

Crab

Mackerel

Octopus

Cod

Angler fish

11. *If attacked, an octopus will try to escape: a) in a cloud of black ink; b) on roller-skates; c) in the sand.*

12. *Can you eat seaweed?*

13. *How many of the sea animals in the picture are fish?*

14. *Fish living 3,000m (10,000ft) down in dark ocean waters can switch on lights. True or false?*

Why do fish need protection?

When too many fish are taken from the sea, fewer fish are available to breed and numbers drop rapidly. Some countries are trying to make international laws to control the numbers of fish caught and to make fishing methods less cruel. Many sea creatures die unnecessarily in nets used to trap other fish. Thousands of dolphins, for instance, have been killed in huge nets called purse seines, used to catch tuna fish.

15. *Dolphins are small whales. True or false?*

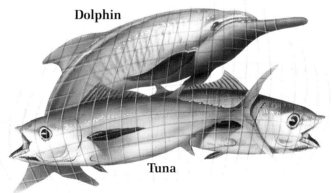

Dolphin

Tuna

People around the world

There are over 5,000 million people in the world. The world's population is now so large that there are more people alive today than have ever lived before. Most live where it is neither too hot nor too cold and there is a good supply of food.

Differences in skin color and face shape developed many thousands of years ago to help people to survive in one particular climate. For example, dark skin protected people in very hot countries from the sun. These differences are not so important today because modern clothes, houses and heating enable people of any physical type to live almost anywhere. Below are three of the most common types, or races, of people.

Negro people originally came from Africa.

1. Which race are Japanese people?

Caucasian people originally came from Europe and Asia.

Mongolian people originally came from Asia.

2. Which race are Scandinavian people?

Where did the first people come from?

People have not always lived all over the world. Scientists believe that the first people came from Africa. They could make tools to hunt with, and fire to keep themselves warm. When their numbers grew these skills enabled them to travel to cooler areas in search of fresh food supplies. The map below shows how people spread to the rest of the world from Africa.

3. The first humans might have hunted: a) camels; b) koalas; c) antelope.

4. No one lives in Antarctica because: a) there are only penguins to eat; b) it is too cold; c) the nightlife is dull.

5. One fifth of the world population today is Chinese. True or false?

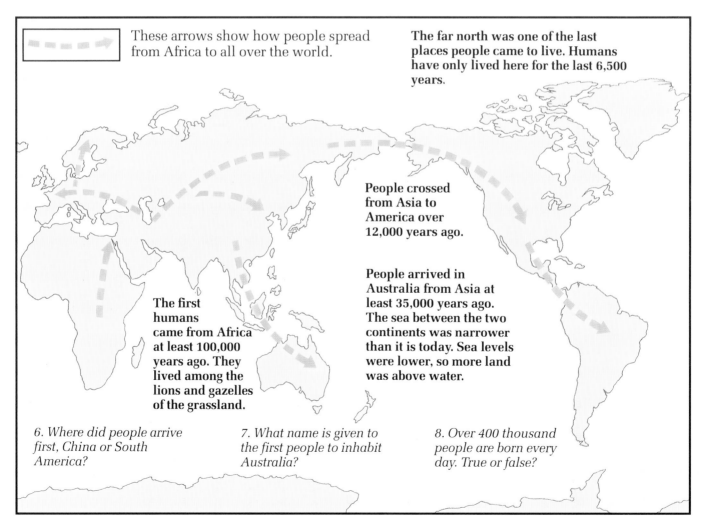

These arrows show how people spread from Africa to all over the world.

The far north was one of the last places people came to live. Humans have only lived here for the last 6,500 years.

People crossed from Asia to America over 12,000 years ago.

The first humans came from Africa at least 100,000 years ago. They lived among the lions and gazelles of the grassland.

People arrived in Australia from Asia at least 35,000 years ago. The sea between the two continents was narrower than it is today. Sea levels were lower, so more land was above water.

6. Where did people arrive first, China or South America?

7. What name is given to the first people to inhabit Australia?

8. Over 400 thousand people are born every day. True or false?

Why do people's lives vary so much?

People live very different lives across the world. Whether a country is rich or poor makes the greatest difference to the quality of everyday life. Religion, language and traditions also influence the way people live.

Families vary in size around the world. In rich countries like the USA, families have an average of two children. Many parents can afford to buy their children expensive clothes and possessions. Many children are encouraged to stay at school and are educated to a high standard.

9. Which of these items do not need electricity?

In poor countries like India, families usually have over six children. In some areas half these children die before they are five. Women have several children to make sure that some survive. Diseases carried in dirty water and sewage are the cause of most childhood deaths. Children cost their parents very little and by the age of 11 or 12 they can work and bring money into the home.

10. Throughout the world an average family has: a) one child; b) four children; c) ten children.

11. Which one of these is essential for any family: a) money; b) food and water; c) television; d) a home?

Did you know?

People in North America and Europe use about forty times as much energy, and eat three times as much food, as people in poor countries in Asia and Africa.

Which country has the most people?

China has the most people. There are over a thousand million Chinese. Two-thirds of them work on farms, which grow enough to feed this huge population. The government encourages couples to have only one child, to stop the population from getting so big it would be impossible to feed.

Rice is the main crop. It grows easily, but needs a lot of water.

A wide hat protects against the hot sun.

Almost all farming is done by hand, rather than with machinery.

12. Which one of these is not a Chinese dish: a) Chow mein; b) Dim sum; c) Shanghai?

How long do people live?

Throughout the world the average lifetime is around 64 years. People currently live the longest in Japan – the world's richest country. Men can expect to live to around 76 and women to around 82.

In Japan people eat a healthy diet. They eat more fish than any other country, and very little fat. Fish is often eaten raw, like this dish on the right, called *sushi*. Health services are good. Most people's lives are stable and comfortable.

Chopsticks

Afghanistan is one country where people have much shorter lives. Few people live beyond forty. War, famine and disease are common and health services are poor.

13. Which continent is Afghanistan in?

How many languages are there?

There are over 5,000 languages in daily use in the world. Mandarin is the most spoken one. It is used by two thirds of the Chinese population – 770 million people. Over 330 million people grow up speaking English, but around 1,000 million people learn it as an additional language. This pie chart represents all the people in the world. It shows how many speak Mandarin, and how many speak English as a first (dark blue) or second (light blue) language.

14. A mandarin is also a type of: a) lemon; b) orange; c) banana; d) grape.

15. The Romans spread the English language around the world. True or false?

Speakers of other languages

Mandarin speakers

English speakers

Cities and towns

The first people on Earth moved from place to place hunting animals and gathering wild fruits and seeds to eat. There were no villages, towns or cities.

About 10,000 years ago, people in some places began to keep animals and grow crops. This enabled them to stay and make homes in one place. These homes were the beginnings of villages, towns and cities. Today, about one third of the world's people live in towns and cities.

1. Which lived on Earth first, dinosaurs or people?

2. Which of these cities was built first: a) Rome; b) Los Angeles; c) Hong Kong?

Tall buildings make the best use of land, which can be expensive in city centers.

What is a city?

A city is a large or important town, where many people live. Thousands more will travel in and out of a big city every day. Some come to work, others to shop or visit professional people such as hospital doctors. Cities are busy, bustling places and city roads are often jammed with traffic – especially when people are traveling to and from work or school. Here are some of the things you might find in a city.

3. Village people might need to visit a town or city to buy: a) bread; b) a newspaper; c) a compact disc.

4. Would cities be cleaner and quieter if everyone came into them on buses and trains, or in their own cars?

5. Put these forms of transport in order of their invention: motorbike, aircraft, train.

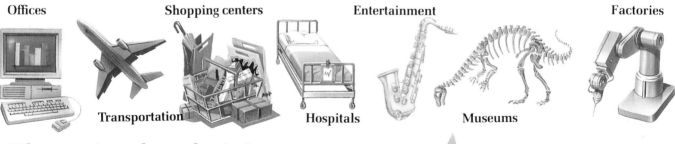

Offices   Shopping centers   Entertainment   Factories

Transportation   Hospitals   Museums

What goes in and out of a city?

A huge amount of food, water and fuel is taken into cities every day. Cities also send out a huge amount of sewage and garbage as well as dirt into the air. The picture on the right shows roughly how much goes into and out of an American city of about a million people each day.

Water 690,000 tons.

Food 2,200 tons.

Fuel for heating, cooking and cars 10,500 tons.

Sewage 550,000 tons.

Refuse 2,200 tons.

Air pollutants 1,100 tons.

6. Chicago, Illinois has nearly three million people. How much food will it need every day?

7. Air pollution is mostly caused by sewage works. True or false?

Where are cities built?

There is always a good reason why a town or city grows up where it does. The picture below shows what some of these reasons might be.

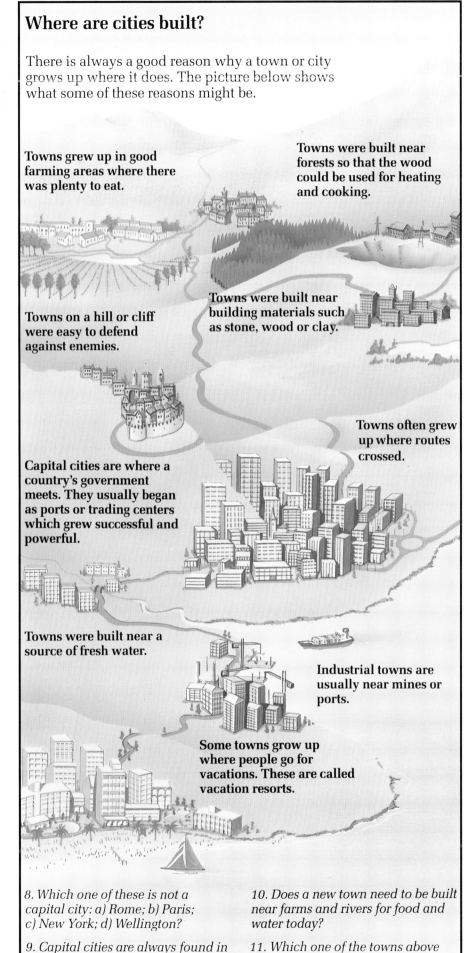

Towns grew up in good farming areas where there was plenty to eat.

Towns were built near forests so that the wood could be used for heating and cooking.

Towns were built near building materials such as stone, wood or clay.

Towns on a hill or cliff were easy to defend against enemies.

Towns often grew up where routes crossed.

Capital cities are where a country's government meets. They usually began as ports or trading centers which grew successful and powerful.

Towns were built near a source of fresh water.

Industrial towns are usually near mines or ports.

Some towns grow up where people go for vacations. These are called vacation resorts.

8. Which one of these is not a capital city: a) Rome; b) Paris; c) New York; d) Wellington?

9. Capital cities are always found in the middle of a country. True or false?

10. Does a new town need to be built near farms and rivers for food and water today?

11. Which one of the towns above would have had most difficulty finding fresh water?

What is a shanty town?

Shanty towns are areas in some cities where the poorest people live. Homes are made from scrap materials like cardboard boxes and corrugated iron. These homes will probably have no gas, drains, electricity or clean water supply. Six or more people may share two small rooms and diseases spread quickly. In Lima, the capital of Peru, one in six people live in a shanty town.

People come to cities such as Lima when they cannot find work in the countryside. They live in shanty towns if they are unable to find a job and a home.

12. Another name for a shanty town is: a) a barriada; b) a boom town; c) a new town.

13. Which continent is Peru in?

Lima has expensive homes too. There is a great difference in the lives of the rich and poor.

14. In some cities homeless children live in sewers. True or false?

Did you know?

The subways in Tokyo are so crowded that special "pushers" are employed to squeeze people into the carriages.

15. Tokyo is the capital city of: a) Mexico; b) Australia; c) Japan.

Spaces and wild places

The empty areas of the Earth are almost always hot, cold or high. Very few people live in these places but those that do have learned how to cope with the extreme conditions.

Many of these people have lived in the same way for thousands of years. This is changing, though. Today, large companies are moving into these areas to look for minerals such as oil, gas and coal. Many wild places can also be turned into farmland.

Who lives in the mountains?

As you go up a mountain, the air gets colder. Fewer plants can grow and only a few types of animal, such as sheep and llamas, can survive.

There is less oxygen the higher up you go. The Quecha Indians live 3,650m (12,000ft) up in the South American Andes. They have bigger hearts and lungs than people living at sea level. These can carry more blood and therefore more oxygen.

1. What are these flat sections cut into the mountainside used for?

2. The Quecha Indians use llamas for: a) transportation; b) pets; c) bed warmers.

Llamas

3. Quecha Indians can walk barefoot over icy rocks without feeling cold. True or false?

Beans and potatoes are tough enough to grow in cold places.

Where are the coldest places?

The coldest places on Earth are the areas within the Arctic and Antarctic Circles round the North and South Poles.

Who lives in the Antarctic?

The continent of Antarctica is covered by a layer of ice three or four kilometres (about two miles) thick. It is too cold for anyone to live a normal life here. Scientists come to study the wildlife or carry out experiments on the air, which is very pure. They live in homes built under the snow, away from the fierce winds and cold.

Outside, the average temperature is –50°C(–58°F).

Entrance

Inside it is 20°C (68°F).

Double door with airlock.

4. Palm trees grow on the coast of Antarctica. True or false?

5. Are polar bears a danger to Antarctic scientists?

Who lives in the Arctic?

Some people live just inside the Arctic circle. The Inuit, for instance, live in northern Canada, Alaska and Greenland. It is warmer here than in Antarctica because inside most of the Arctic Circle is ocean, which is warmer than land. Near the North Pole, though, the Arctic Ocean is frozen solid.

6. Which one of these countries does not have land inside the Arctic Circle: a) Greenland; b) Canada; c) Scotland?

7. Do the Inuit all live in igloos?

These traditional Inuit clothes are made of animal skins. Many Inuit now wear clothing made from man-made materials.

Thick skin jacket.

Thick sealskin or reindeer skin trousers.

Strong sealskin boots stuffed with dry grass.

The Inuit are mostly short and stocky. This helps them to keep warm as there is less body area exposed to the cold than in tall, long-limbed people. Many Inuit now work in the local oil and gas industries instead of making a living by hunting and fishing in the traditional way.

Who lives in deserts?

Deserts are areas with little or no rain. People who live in them have to be able to survive when there is very little food or water. The San of the Kalahari desert live by hunting animals and gathering plants.

The San live in small groups of 20 people or less. They camp for only a few weeks in one place. From each camp they hunt and gather over an area of 600 sq km (230 sq miles). Today, much of the San's richer land has been taken over by wealthy cattle ranchers.

The San make cloaks, called karosses, from animal skins to keep them warm at night.

They have few possessions to carry with them.

8. Is it hot or cold at night in the desert?

The San search for water-filled plants such as tsama melons. These may be the only source of water for up to nine months of the year. San women's bodies adapt themselves so that they do not get pregnant when there is a drought.

Tsama melons

The San eat every scrap of meat killed in a hunt. They can store more fat on their bodies than most people.

The San hunt with bows and arrows.

9. In droughts, San only hunt male animals. True or false?

Did you know?

The San store water in ostrich eggshells. They sometimes bury the shells, so that they can use the water when rivers and water holes dry up. The eggshells are around 1cm (1/2in) thick, so they are quite tough.

10. Which are bigger, ostrich eggs or hen eggs?

What is a tropical rainforest?

Tropical rainforests grow near the Equator where it is very hot and wet. They are the home of nearly half the world's different kinds of plants and animals.

The soil in a rainforest is kept rich by dead leaves and rotting wood from the trees. If the forest is cut down the soil loses its goodness and can no longer be used for growing crops. People who live in the forest survive by looking after it.

11. About two million different kinds of plants and animals live in rainforests. True or false?

Who lives in the rainforest?

The Mbuti pygmies of Central Africa live by hunting wild animals and gathering edible plants. They move from place to place in search of food. They do no damage to the forest.

12. Are pygmies short or tall people?

13. Which people have a bigger choice of food, the San or the Mbuti?

Women and girls build houses. They cover a stick framework with a layer of large leaves.

Honey **Nuts**

Yam

14. A yam is a vegetable which tastes like: a) a potato; b) a carrot; c) a cabbage.

15. It takes about: a) a week; b) a day; c) five minutes to build a pygmy house.

Today, the forest is being cleared for farmland and timber. This is taking away land from the pygmies. Many now work as farm laborers in villages at the edge of the forest.

Using the land

Two out of three people on Earth live and work on farms. They grow food, or crops such as rubber and cotton. The land is farmed in many different ways. Some people only grow enough to feed themselves and their families. Others have huge areas of land where crops such as wheat are grown. These crops are sold to large companies who then sell them all over the world.

1. Which two of the following are made from wheat: a) corn flakes; b) bread; c) spaghetti; d) rice pudding?

2. Which one of the following foods is not farmed: a) beef; b) trout; c) apples; d) tuna; e) rice?

Who are the small farmers?

Most farms in poor countries are small. Many people only have enough land to grow food for themselves. Some farmers also keep farms small to protect the soil. In tropical rainforests, for example, the soil would be destroyed if large areas of forest were cut to make fields.

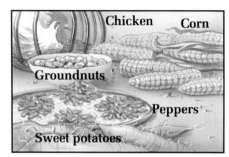

The Yanomami of South America clear small gardens in the tropical rainforest. Some trees are left to protect the soil. After two or three years the garden is left to return to forest and a new area is cleared.

3. Sometimes a Yanomamo person is eaten by monkeys. True or false?

The Tuareg of the Sahara keep herds of camels and goats, to provide them with milk and meat. They need to travel from place to place to find enough food to feed their animals.

4. The Sahara is a huge desert in South America. True or false?

On some small farms, the farmers grow more than they need to feed themselves. They sell the extra at local markets. The picture shows the kinds of food you could buy in a Nigerian market.

5. In which continent is Nigeria?

Why are some farms so big?

In richer countries, where most people work in towns and cities, farmland is likely to be owned by only a few farmers. Most of these farms cover large areas of land. Some farms grow a single type of crop, or keep just one breed of animal. In the USA, grain is grown in huge fields. Expensive machines do most of the work and very few people work on the farm.

Wheat farm in central USA.

Merino sheep. These are reared for their fine wool, on huge sheep farms in Australia.

6. The farm machine shown above is: a) a combine harvester; b) a plow; c) a crop sprayer.

7. Are there more sheep-farmers or sheep-shearers in Australia?

Some Australian sheep farms are so huge that farmers travel around their farms in small planes.

8. Which of these countries is also well-known for its sheep: a) Peru; b) New Zealand; c) Finland?

What is a plantation?

Plantations are large estates where one crop, such as coffee, cocoa, tea or rubber, is grown. Most plantation crops need to be picked by hand, and many people work on plantations for low wages.

More than one third of the farmland in poor countries is used for plantations. They produce crops to be sold to other countries. Many plantation workers have their own plot of land to grow food for themselves.

9. Bananas grow underground. True or false?

10. Which of these countries is not a major tea producer: a) China; b) India; c) Belgium?

Cocoa beans are used to make chocolate.

Tea leaves are picked by hand.

Coffee beans are inside coffee berries.

Where does your food come from?

The food you eat comes from all over the world. Different kinds of food need different kinds of climate. Coffee grows well in Brazil and Kenya, for example. These countries usually have a very hot climate and a lot of rain. Apples, though, like a warm climate, as in France, and medium amounts of rain. The map below shows some examples of where your food might come from.

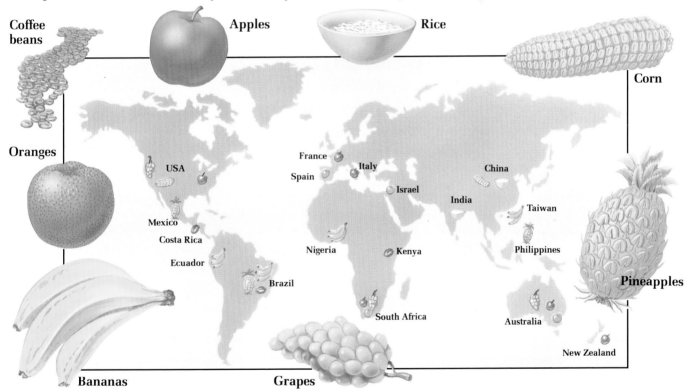

Coffee beans — Apples — Rice — Corn

Oranges

France, Spain, Italy, Israel, USA, Mexico, Costa Rica, Ecuador, Brazil, Nigeria, Kenya, South Africa, China, India, Taiwan, Philippines, Australia, New Zealand

Pineapples

Bananas — Grapes

11. Can bananas be farmed in parts of Europe?

12. Are there farms in all seven continents?

13. Do dates grow best in warm or cold countries?

Did you know?

Potatoes and many other common foods were unknown in Europe until the sixteenth century. Explorers brought them back from the mountains in the northern Andes, in South America. Explorers also brought tobacco, tomatoes and chilies from America to Europe.

14. South American Indians worshipped the potato. True or false?

15. Which one of these is not needed in a balanced diet: a) carbohydrate; b) protein; c) meat; d) vitamins; e) minerals?

Fuel and energy

Anything that lives or moves needs energy. A car needs fuel to drive its engine. You need food to give your body energy.

Energy in fuels such as coal, oil and gas can be converted into electricity by burning and processing them in power stations. You can use this electricity for lighting, heating, cooking and many other things. Most ways of producing electricity cause pollution*, and new ways are being developed that are cleaner and safer.

How was coal made?

About 300 million years ago large areas of the Earth were covered in hot, wet, tropical swamps.

As plants died, they collected in the bottom of the swamps.

Over millions of years, layers of sand and clay settled on top. They pressed down and hardened into rocks.

The pressure from the rocks gradually changed the plants into peat and then into coal.

When coal is burned, it produces gases which make the air dirty. This is called air pollution (see pages 24-25).

1. Is coal found only underground?

2. Do trees contain energy?

What are fossil fuels?

Fossil fuels are fuels such as coal and oil which are found buried below the land and sea. They are made from the remains of animals and plants which lived millions of years ago. They contain energy which was stored by the animals and plants when they were alive.

3. Which of these is not a fossil fuel: a) oil; b) wood; c) coal?

When will fossil fuels run out?

Fossil fuels will not last forever. The world's coal supplies will probably run out in about 400 years. Oil and gas supplies will probably run out by the middle of the next century. There are plenty of energy sources on Earth besides fossil fuels. Some of them are shown below.

You can see how the energy is released from these sources on the next page. This sort of energy is called renewable or free energy because it will never run out.

4. Where is natural gas found?

5. Oil is found underground in: a) oil mines; b) oil wells; c) oil barrels.

What is nuclear energy?

You, and everything in the world, are made from atoms. Atoms are so tiny that there are more atoms in an ant than there are people in the world. Nuclear energy is made from splitting the atoms of a metal called uranium. When the center, or nucleus, is split, heat is given off. This can be used to make electricity.

6. A piece of uranium the size of a pin contains as much energy as 5,500 tons of coal. True or false?

7. Put these in order of discovery: a) steam power; b) nuclear power; c) electricity.

This picture shows how an atom is split.

A tiny particle, called a neutron, is fired at the uranium nucleus.

Uranium nucleus

* There is more about pollution on pages 24-25.

What is the energy of the future?

The pictures below show several ways of supplying energy which do not depend on fossil fuels.

Solar panel

Windmill

Windmill blades turn turbines to make electricity. One hundred windmills could provide enough electricity for 400,000 people.

Solar panels trap the Sun's heat. This heats water to make steam to run turbines in power stations. Solar power can also be used to heat houses.

8. It costs nothing to convert free energy into electricity.
True or false?

Tidal power dam

The movement of the tide can be used to turn turbines and make electricity, by building a tidal power dam across an estuary.

9. Is tidal power made inland or by the sea?

10. Do bicycles, skateboards and horse-drawn carts need fuel to make them move?

11. Which is the best source of energy for hot desert countries?

12. Which one of these uses energy from water: a) steam train; b) yacht; c) aircraft?

13. Which is the best source of energy for flat, windy countries?

Are there other energy sources?

These sources of energy are also being developed.

Biogas is a gas made from rotting animal, plant and human waste. A small farm can provide itself with enough biogas to cook with.

There is a lot of heat energy inside the Earth. In Iceland and New Zealand, hot springs heat homes and make electricity.

Chains of rafts around a coastline absorb the energy of waves and turn it into electricity.

The power in falling water can be used to make electricity.

14. What is electricity made from the power in falling water called?

Many kinds of household and industrial garbage, which is usually buried, can be burned, and the heat used to make electricity. This also gets rid of the garbage. However, burning garbage does cause air pollution.

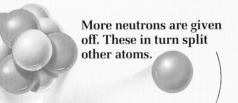

More neutrons are given off. These in turn split other atoms.

The nucleus is split and heat is given off.

Neutrons

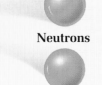

When an atom is split, it sends harmful, invisible rays into the air. This is called radiation. It can cause burns and cancer. The waste from nuclear fuel is also radioactive (it gives off harmful radiation). No one has yet found a completely safe way to get rid of this waste.

Did you know?

It is possible to run a car on alcohol. In Brazil, an alcohol called ethanol is made from sugar cane. Ethanol burns easily and can be used for fuel in cars with modified engines. In 1990 a third of all cars in Brazil ran on ethanol.

15. Cars can also run on cow dung.
True or false?

Pollution

When air, water or land is made dirty or poisonous it is described as polluted. A polluted environment can be very harmful to the people, animals and plants within it.

1. Which of these cause pollution: a) planes; b) bicycles; c) cars; d) sailing dinghies?

What is acid rain?

Acid rain is made when poisonous gases and smoke in the air mix with water droplets in the clouds. This makes weak acids which fall to the ground as acid rain. This is sour, like vinegar, and it can kill plants and fish. The pictures below show where most of the poisonous gases that make acid rain come from.

Burning fossil fuels in power stations.

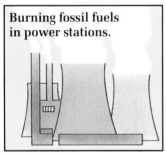

Burning fuel in factories, to drive machinery.

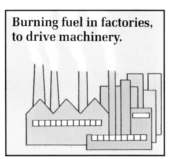

Exhaust fumes from cars, trucks and buses.

Burning fuel for cooking and heating in homes.

2. Is there such a thing as acid snow?

3. Can you name two ways of producing electrical energy which do not pollute the air?

What is the ozone layer?

Ozone is a gas which occurs 20-50km (10-30 miles) above the ground and forms a protective layer around the Earth.

6. Is the ozone layer above or below where the weather happens?

Ozone protects the Earth from dangerous light rays, called ultra-violet light, in sunlight. Too much ultra-violet light can cause skin cancer and eye diseases as well as damaging food crops, fish and other sea life.

7. Ultra-violet light can turn your skin purple. True or false?

The ozone layer is being damaged by gases called CFCs (short for chlorofluorocarbons, pronounced kloro-floro-carbons). These are used in things like foam boxes for take-away food, and in refrigerators and air-conditioning units. When these things break down or are destroyed, CFCs are released into the atmosphere.

Ozone layer wraps around the Earth.

Hole in ozone layer

Ultra-violet rays

Scientists have discovered two huge holes in the ozone layer – one over the Antarctic as big as the USA and another over the Arctic as big as Greenland.

8. Which of these might contain CFCs: a) cereal packet; b) hamburger carton; c) paper bag?

What harm does acid rain do?

Clouds containing acid rain may be carried more than 1,000km (over 600 miles) by the wind. The acid rain then falls a long way from the city, factory or power station which caused it. Acid rain can affect the environment in several ways, as shown in the pictures below.

Acid rain damages plants and crops. It removes the richness from the soil so crops cannot grow well.

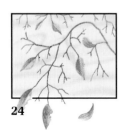

Acid rain attacks leaves on trees. Half of western Germany's forests are dying due to acid rain.

Acid rain pollutes water. About 4,000 lakes in Sweden now have no fish due to poisoning by acid rain.

Acid rain eats away at buildings. It is a particularly damaging type of air pollution. An Ancient Greek temple called the Parthenon has been worn down more in the last 30 years than in the last 2,000.

Acid rain eats into buildings.

The Parthenon

4. The Parthenon is in: a) Rome; b) Athens; c) Cairo.

5. The Parthenon is made of concrete. True or false?

Sun's rays

What is the greenhouse effect?

A certain kind of air pollution is making the Earth's atmosphere act like a greenhouse. It is making the Earth's temperature rise very slowly. The Sun warms up the Earth but the atmosphere does not let the heat escape into space. This is called the greenhouse effect. It is also called global warming.

9. Only green plants grow in greenhouses. True or false?

Carbon dioxide acts like a greenhouse around the Earth.

The main cause of global warming is too much carbon dioxide in the atmosphere. Fossil fuels give off carbon dioxide when they are burned. Power stations which use coal are big producers of carbon dioxide. Fumes from car exhausts and CFCs also add to global warming.

In a greenhouse, the Sun shines through the glass and heats the air. The glass stops most of the heat from leaving the greenhouse.

10. Carbon dioxide in the atmosphere acts like the: a) glass; b) plants; c) air in a greenhouse.

11. Which one of these can help stop global warming: a) planting forests; b) burning fossil fuels; c) building greenhouses?

Why is global warming a problem?

If the world heats up by just a few degrees, some of the ice around the North and South Poles will melt. The extra water in the oceans will make sea levels slowly rise all over the world. Cities such as London and New York could disappear under the sea. Low-lying countries like Holland and Bangladesh could disappear completely.

Existing coastline

Coastline after rise in sea level

The pictures on the left show how the map of Western Europe would change if all the ice at the poles were to melt. The sea would rise by 61m (200 ft).

13. Which two of these could cause flooding in a country: a) tidal waves; b) monsoon rain; c) severe drought; d) overflowing baths?

12. Would you use a physical or a political map to work out how a rise in sea level would affect the land?

Did you know?

If a plastic bottle is dumped in the countryside, it will stay there for ever. Sunlight will decompose the plastic a little but once the bottle is buried in the ground it will not rot any more.

14. Which one of these everyday items cannot be made out of plastic: a) reading glasses; b) raincoat; c) ham sandwich; d) carpet; e) carrier bag?

15. Which of these words means "to use again": a) recycle; b) reset; c) reserve?

How can pollution be reduced?

Here are some of the ways you can help to reduce pollution.

Use less electricity. Switch off lights and heaters when you do not need them. If you have a short journey, walk instead of travelling by car.	**These will help reduce gases which cause acid rain and global warming.**
Use laundry detergents which do not contain phosphate cleaning chemicals. Use smaller amounts of dishwashing liquid and scouring powder.	**All these cleaners pollute water.**
Make sure that all your trash goes in the trash can, not in the street or countryside. If you can, buy glass or tin containers rather than plastic, and recycle them.	**Glass and tin can be broken down and used again. Many plastics are indestructible.**

Megaquiz

These ten quizzes test you on what you have read in this book and also on your general knowledge of geography.

You can write your answers on a piece of paper and then check on page 32 to see how many you got right.

Capitals and countries

Can you match the capital cities in the mauve strip to the countries in the blue strip?

Canada	New Zealand	India	Denmark	Argentina	USA	Australia	China	Spain	Peru

Delhi	Copenhagen	Buenos Aires	Ottawa	Wellington	Beijing	Madrid	Lima	Washington DC	Canberra

Earth facts

1. Which is the largest ocean?
2. Which is the most southern continent?
3. Latitude and longitude lines are found:
   a) on the sides of mountains; b) on maps;
   c) on fishing boats.
4. Which is the thinnest layer of the Earth:
   a) the crust; b) the mantle; c) the core?
5. How long does it take for the Earth to spin around once on its axis?
6. Glaciers are frozen: a) lakes; b) waterfalls; c) rivers.
7. Are tropical rainforests getting larger or smaller?
8. Is more of the Earth covered by sea or by land?
9. Where might you find phytoplankton:
   a) in the sea; b) under the ground; c) in the atmosphere?
10. What is the name of latitude 0°?

Seas and oceans

Can you match the seas and oceans in the list below with the areas marked a – j on the map?

Atlantic Ocean
Antarctic Ocean
Indian Ocean
Pacific Ocean
Black Sea

North Sea
Arctic Ocean
South China Sea
Arabian Sea
Mediterranean Sea

People and places

Can you match the people described below to the shaded places on the map?

1. The first people on Earth probably lived here, according to scientists.
2. People here currently have the longest lives.
3. The Tuareg live in this desert.
4. The Inuit live here.
5. The San live in this desert.
6. The Yanomami live in this rainforest.
7. The Quecha Indians live in these mountains.
8. People in this country form the largest population.
9. People crossed from Asia to this continent 12,000 years ago.
10. Over a fifth of the world can speak the language of the people from this country.

Close-ups

These are all close-ups of pictures in the book. Can you recognize what they are?

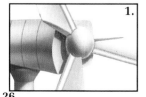 1.
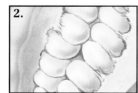 2.
 3.
 4.
 5.

Countries and continents

Match the pictures of countries and continents labeled a – j to the list of places below.

Australia   Japan   South America
Italy   Canada   Antarctica
Greece   Norway   Africa
India

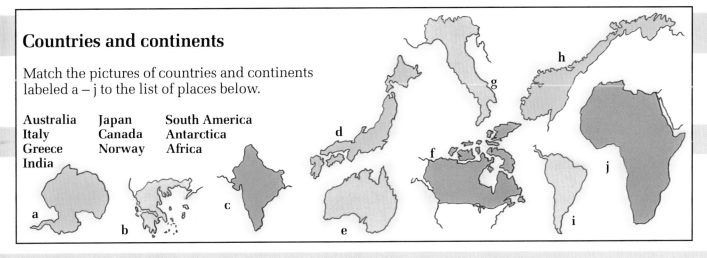

The sky and beyond

1. The first person landed on the Moon in:
   a) 1928; b) 1969; c) 1989.
2. The Moon takes about: a) a day; b) a week;
   c) a month to circle the Earth.
3. Which part of the environment do CFCs harm:
   a) the ozone layer; b) the sea; c) the soil?
4. Which planet is closest to the Sun?
5. Does lightning make the air it goes through hot
   or cold?
6. Is the Sun; a) a planet; b) a star; c) an
   asteroid?
7. Which is bigger, the Universe or our solar
   system?
8. Which of these is not usually found in the air:
   a) oxygen; b) nitrogen; c) plutonium?
9. What is a mixture of falling ice and rain called?
10. Which is bigger, a hurricane or a tornado?

Misfits

In each set of three below, there is one misfit. Can you spot which it is?

1. Jupiter; Saturn; the Moon.
2. Brazil; Tokyo; Sweden.
3. Mediterranean; Pacific; Atlantic.
4. Tornado; hurricane; lightning.
5. Quecha; San; Merino.
6. Wood; coal; oil.
7. Wave power; wind power; nuclear power.
8. Cirrus; axis; stratus.
9. Alabama; Andes; Alps.
10. Sahara; Kalahari; Nairobi.

Silhouettes

All these silhouettes are of things that appear in the book. How many can you recognize?

True or false?

1. The Moon circles around the Earth.
2. Some mountain people have bigger hearts and lungs
   than people living at sea level.
3. Saturn's rings are made of gold.
4. Scientists have traveled to the center of the Earth.
5. Most of the people in the world live or work on
   farms.
6. A country is a small continent.
7. Thunder is caused by two clouds bumping into each
   other.
8. The Earth is traveling through space at nearly
   30km (18.6 miles) per second.
9. Some cars can run on sugar.
10. Asteroids are a drug for fattening cattle.

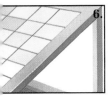   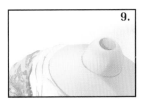 

Quiz answers

The answers to the 12 quizzes from *The Earth in Space* to *Pollution* are on the next four pages. Give yourself one point for every right answer. The chart below helps you find out how well you have done in each quiz.

0-5	Read through the answers, then try the quiz again. See how many answers you can remember second time around.	11-14	Good score. If you get this score on most of the quizzes, you have done very well.
6-10	Quite good. Think more carefully about the questions and you might get more answers right.	15	Excellent. If you do this well in more than half the quizzes, you are a geography genius!

Your score overall

You can find out your average score over all 12 quizzes like this:

1. Add up your scores on all 12 quizzes.
2. Divide this total by 12. This is your average score. How well did you do?

General knowledge

All the answers to general knowledge questions are marked★. These questions are probably the hardest in the quizzes. Add up how many of them you got right across all 12 quizzes. There are 50 of them in total. If you got over 30 right, your geography general knowledge is good.

The Earth's atmosphere

1. c) A solar system is made up of a star and circling planets.
★ 2. No. The Earth is just one tiny planet in one of millions of galaxies.
★ 3. a) light years. A light year is the distance a ray of light would travel in a year – 9,460 thousand million km (5,878 thousand million miles).
4. No. Stars give off light and heat. The Moon only reflects sunlight.
★ 5. b) Neil Armstrong was the first man on the Moon, in July 1969.

Neil Armstrong's landing craft.

6. Pluto is the coldest planet, as it is the farthest (5,900 million km or 3,700 million miles) from the Sun.
★ 7. Venus is named after the Roman goddess of love.
8. The Milky Way is much bigger than a solar sytem.
9. JUPITER and MARS.
10. In the picture when it is day in Africa it is night in South America.
11. True. In July the top of the Earth is tilting toward the Sun. The North Pole never moves into the area of shadow.

North Pole — **Earth's axis** — **Sun's rays**

12. False. All parts of the world have 24 hours in a day.
13. No. In our solar system, Mercury and Venus do not have moons.
14. No. Neptune is a very cold planet with a poisonous, frozen atmosphere. Nothing could survive there.
15. No. You cannot see a New Moon because the side of it that is lit up is facing away from the Earth.

The surface of the Earth

1. The Arctic and Antarctic would be white or bluish-white. They are both covered with ice and snow.
★ 2. The largest continent is Asia.

Asia

Australia is the smallest continent.

3. No. Nobody lives at the North Pole. It is in the frozen Arctic Ocean.
4. False. Cold weather and steep slopes make mountains difficult to farm.
★ 5. The Himalayas are in Asia.
6. There are many more penguins than people at the Antarctic.
7. True. The Sahara desert covers almost all of northern Africa.
8. b) The River Nile flows through Egypt.
9. True. Around two-thirds of Brazil is covered by the Amazon rainforest.

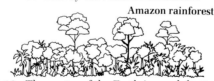
Amazon rainforest

★10. The center of the Earth is much hotter than the Sahara desert. It is probably about 6,000°C (11,000°F) at the center of the Earth – over one hundred times hotter than any temperature recorded on land.
★11. True. Africa and South America used to be joined together. They began to separate about 135 million years ago.
12. a) The lowest places on Earth are at the bottom of the sea. The lowest place known is the Marianas Trench which is more than 11,000m (36,000ft) below sea level.
13. b) San Francisco is famous for its earthquakes.
★14. Yes. Volcanoes can erupt under the sea as well as on land.
★15. Mount Everest. It is 8,848m (29,028ft) high.

Mapping the world

1. A globe is more accurate than a flat map of the Earth. Map-makers do not need to change the shapes of the land and sea to make a globe.

Globe

★ 2. Asia is the missing continent.
3. You would use a political map to find a country's borders. Political maps usually also show the position of major cities.
4. There are 13 countries in South America. These are: Argentina; Bolivia; Brazil; Chile; Columbia; Ecuador; French Guiana; Guyana; Paraguay; Peru; Surinam; Uraguay and Venezuela.
5. No. There is not a West Pole (or an East Pole).
★ 6. The direction half way between north and east is north-east.
★ 7. South is the direction at the bottom of most maps.
8. No. Latitude and longitude lines are only found on maps.
9. c) London. Longitude 0° runs through an astronomy museum, called the Royal Observatory, and is marked on the floor with an iron bar.

Greenwich Royal Observatory

10. The ships are nearer to Europe.
11. The volcano's position is 40°N, 20°E.
12. The hurricane's position is 20°N 60°W.
13. There is flat land on the map at C.
14. It is very steep at B.
15. A is at the top of a hill.

The Earth's atmosphere

★ 1. You need to breathe oxygen.
2. Yes. Jets cruise above most weather, but still have to fly through bad weather when they take off and land.
★ 3. b) At 0km (0 miles) it is sea level. This is the same everywhere, unlike land with its mountains and valleys.
4. True. There is less air above you on top of a mountain than there is at sea level, so air pressure is less.
★ 5. It is hot at the Equator. The Sun's rays are most concentrated here.

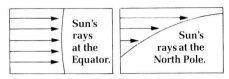

| Sun's rays at the Equator. | Sun's rays at the North Pole. |

★ 6. a) A weather vane tells you which way the wind is blowing.

Weather vane

7. False. It is warmer at sea level than on the top of a mountain. This is because the Sun's rays have more land surface area to heat in mountainous areas than in flat ground and sea. Also, air holds heat, and the higher you go, the less air there is to hold it.

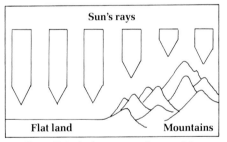

Sun's rays

Flat land   Mountains

8. Great Britain has more changeable weather than the Sahara desert, which is hot and dry all through the year.
9. No. Climate is the kind of weather a place has on average year after year. Weather is what a place has from day to day.
10. Cirrus clouds are the highest clouds. They are found at around 18km (11 miles) up in the sky.
★ 11. c) Smog is a mixture of smoke and fog.
12. The storm is about 4km (2 miles) away if you hear thunder ten seconds after seeing lightning.
13. There are more thunderstorms at the Equator. Weather here is far more changeable, with plenty of the hot air currents thunderstorms need.
14. True. The center of a hurricane is called the eye. The eye is a calm area with no wind.
15. False. Tornadoes have never been known to lift trains right off the ground. They can, however, turn over trains and grounded aircraft.

Rivers and rain

1. a) Camels can survive without a drink for 21 days (three weeks) if they only eat dry food. If they eat succulent desert plants which contain water, they never need to drink.

Desert plant

2. b) The water in wet laundry becomes water vapor when it dries.
3. Clouds are made of water. Most clouds are made of tiny water droplets, but high cirrus clouds have tiny ice crystals in them.
4. True. In fact all the water in the world is constantly being recycled.
5. Yes. Your breath contains water vapor. You can see the water in your breath when you breathe out on a cold day.
★ 6. a) The Thames (346km/215 miles) is much shorter than either the Nile (6670km/4145 miles) or Amazon (6448 km/4007 miles). The Nile is the longest river in the world.

Relative length of rivers:

Thames —

Amazon ————————————

Nile   ————————————

7. False. Rivers can only flow downhill.
★ 8. Water freezes at 0°C (32°F).
9. b) You can live without water for four days.
10. False. Hydroelectric power stations are often found in mountainous regions where fast flowing water drives the power station turbines.
11. Hydroelectric, tidal and wave power are all forms of water power.
★ 12. b) The Grand Canyon is not a famous waterfall. It is a deep, steep-sided valley, cut by the Colorado River in the USA.

The Grand Canyon

13. True. Fish caught from polluted rivers and eaten can cause stomach upsets or more serious poisoning.
14. c) Glaciers are found in Scandinavia. Glaciers are also found in many other parts of the world, such as India, where there are high mountains.
15. Rivers flow a lot quicker than glaciers. Glaciers only move a few centimetres (an inch or two) a day, so slowly that you cannot see them move.

Oceans and coasts

1. Yes. The Earth's oceans are all joined together.
2. c) The Mediterranean is a sea.

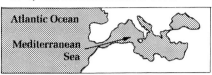

★ 3. Yes. Seawater evaporates in shallow pools and salt is left behind.
4. True. Seawater contains a tiny amount of gold.
5. True. In big storms cliffs can form overnight. In 1953 at Covehithe in England the coast was cut back 27m (90ft) in a day.
6. False. Cliffs can also be found along river banks where the river has worn away the valley in its path.
★ 7. a) A starling is not a seabird.
8. Sand dunes are found on beaches. They occur when the wind usually blows in the direction of the shore and sand is blown up the beach.

Wind   Sand dune

9. c) You can see about one eighth of an iceberg above the water.

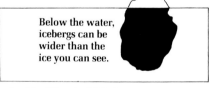

Below the water, icebergs can be wider than the ice you can see.

★ 10. The Titanic. This luxury passenger liner was traveling from England to the USA. When the Titanic sank, over 1,500 people drowned.
11. a) An octopus will try to escape from an enemy in a cloud of black ink. The octopus carries this ink, called sepia, in a special sac in its body. Artists have used sepia in paintings since Roman times.
12. Yes, seaweed such as laver, dulse, and sea lettuce can be eaten.

Edible seaweed

★ 13. Three of these animals are fish – the mackerel, cod and angler fish.
14. True. Many deep sea fish have parts of their bodies which light up. The light comes from luminous bacteria, which live in the fish. These lights attract prey to eat, and also other deep sea fish to mate with.
15. True. Dolphins are small streamlined whales.

People around the world

1. Japanese people are of the Mongolian race.
2. Scandinavian people are of the Caucasian race.
3. c) The first humans might have hunted antelope in the African grassland.
4. b) No one lives permanently in Antarctica because it is too cold.

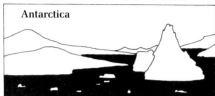
Antarctica

5. True. About one in five people on Earth are Chinese.
6. People arrived in China first. There have been people in China for at least 70,000 years. Scientists think that people only reached South America around 11,000 years ago.
★ 7. The original inhabitants of Australia are called Aborigines.
8. True. Around 400,000 babies are born every day. Around 150,000 people die every day too, so each day there are 250,000 more people on Earth.

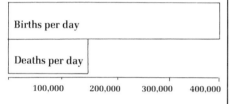

Births per day			
Deaths per day			
100,000	200,000	300,000	400,000

9. The tennis racket and the books do not need electricity. Electrical power has only been widely available since the beginning of this century.
10. b) Throughout the world the average number of children in a family is four.
11. b) Food and water are essential for survival.
★ 12. c) Shanghai is not a Chinese dish, it is a city in China. Beijing is China's capital city, but Shanghai is its biggest city, and largest port.

CHINA Beijing •
Shanghai •

★ 13. Afghanistan is in the continent of Asia.

EUROPE
Afghanistan
ASIA
AFRICA

★ 14. b) orange.
15. False. The Romans spoke Latin.

Cities and towns

★ 1. Dinosaurs lived on Earth first. They died out about 65 million years ago. The first people lived on Earth less than one million years ago.

Dinosaur

2. a) Rome was built first, over 2,500 years ago.
3. c) Village people might need to visit a town or city to buy a compact disc.
4. Cities would be cleaner and quieter if everyone came into them on buses and trains.
★ 5. The right order is train, motorbike, aircraft.

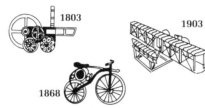
1803   1903
1868

6. Chicago would need about 6,600 tons of food every day.
7. False. Air pollution is mostly caused by industry, power stations burning fossil fuels, and cars.
8. c) New York. The capital of the USA is Washington DC.
9. False. Capital cities may be anywhere in a country. For example, Madrid, the capital of Spain, is in the center of the country, but Washington DC is on the east coast of the USA.

Madrid
Washington • DC

10. No. Water can be piped and food transported over huge distances, so new towns can be built almost anywhere.
11. The town that has been built upon a hill to defend itself from enemies would have had the most difficulty finding fresh water.
12. a) A barriada is another name for a shanty town.
★ 13. Peru is in the continent of South America.

Pacific Ocean   Atlantic Ocean
Peru   SOUTH AMERICA

14. True. For example, in Brazil in South America, there are homeless children who live in sewers.
15. c) Tokyo is the capital city of Japan.

Spaces and wild places

★ 1. The flat sections cut into the mountainside are used for growing food. They are called terraces and they stop soil from being washed away.
2. a) The Quecha Indians use llamas for transport.
3. True. The Quechas' feet become toughened so they do not feel cold.
4. False. Palm trees only grow in warm climates.

Palm trees

★ 5. No. Polar bears do not live in the Antarctic. Like walruses, they are only found in the Arctic.
★ 6. c) Scotland does not have land within the Arctic Circle.
7. No. Very few Inuit still live in igloos, although some Inuit build them on winter hunting trips.

Igloo

8. It is cold at night in deserts. The temperature can drop below freezing.
9. True. In a drought the San take care not to hurt female and young animals so that some animals will survive for another time.
★ 10. Ostrich eggs are much bigger than hen eggs. An ostrich egg can be 20cm (8in) long and 15cm (6in) around.

Ostrich egg
Hen egg

11. True. There are more varieties of plants and animals in tropical rainforests than anywhere else on Earth.
★ 12. Pygmies are short people. Men in pygmy tribes are usually less than 150cm (5ft) tall.
13. The Mbuti have a bigger choice of food than the San. The rainforest provides the Mbuti with nuts, roots, vegetables and fungi, as well as termites, freshwater crabs and animals like antelope.
★ 14. a) A yam is a vegetable which tastes like a potato.

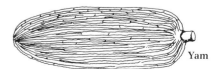
Yam

15. b) It takes about a day to make a pygmy house.

Using the land

1. b) and c). Bread and spaghetti are made from wheat.

Wheat

2. d) Tuna are not farmed. Tuna are fished from the open ocean, using large nets.
3. False. However, the Yanomami do sometimes eat monkeys.
4. False. The Sahara desert is a huge desert in Africa. It is about as big as the USA.
5. Nigeria is in the continent of Africa.

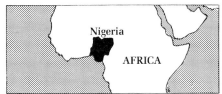

Nigeria

AFRICA

6. a) The farm machine shown in the picture is a combine harvester. Combine harvesters are used to cut wheat and other crops. They cut the straw and separate it from the grain. The grain is stored in the machine and the straw is dropped out of the back of the machine.
7. There are more shearers than sheep farmers in Australia. Each sheep is sheared by hand and shearers travel from farm to farm.
8. b) New Zealand is also well-known for its sheep.
9. False. Bananas grow on huge herb plants which look like trees.

Banana plant

10. c) Belgium is not a major tea producer. Belgium is too cold for growing tea.
11. No. Bananas need a hot, wet, tropical climate to grow well.
12. No. There are no farms in Antarctica.
13. Dates grow best in warm countries.

Dates

14. False. South American Indians grew potatoes for food.
★15. c) Meat is not needed in a balanced diet. However, meat is a good source of protein, vitamins and minerals.

Fuel and energy

★ 1. No. Coal is not found only underground. Layers, or seams, of coal can be found on the surface and on the sides of hills. Collecting coal from these seams is called "open-cast mining".

Digger used in open-cast mining.

2. Yes. The energy in trees is released when they are burned for heating or cooking.
3. b) Wood is not a fossil fuel.
★ 4. Natural gas is found underground. It is often found with or near oil.

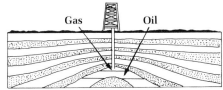

Gas   Oil

★ 5. b) Oil is found underground in oil wells.
6. True.
★ 7. Beginning with the earliest, the order is: a) steam power (early 18th century); c) electric power (late 19th century); b) nuclear power (mid-20th century).

Light bulb 1879

8. False. It is expensive to build power stations and turbines to convert free energy to electricity. Once completed, however, they are inexpensive to run.
9. Tidal power is made by the sea. A dam is usually built across a tidal river estuary.
★10. Yes. Even though skateboards, horse-drawn carts and bicycles do not use fuel, they still need energy. This comes from the food that the cyclist, skateboarder and horse eat.
11. The best source of energy for desert countries is solar energy, as the Sun shines nearly all the time.
12. a) Steam trains convert water to steam, which powers their wheels.
13. Wind to drive windmills is the best source of energy for flat, windy countries.

Wind farm in California.

★14. This kind of electricity is called hydroelectricity.
15. False. Dried cow dung can be used, however, as a fuel for heating and cooking.

Pollution

1. a) and c). Plane and car engines burn fossil fuels, which cause pollution.
2. Yes. Acid snow is made in a similar way as acid rain.
★ 3. Give yourself a point if you got two of the following: hydroelectric power, wave power, tidal power, wind power, solar power, underground heat.
★ 4. b) The Parthenon is in Athens.

GREECE

Athens

5. False. The Parthenon was built of white marble, nearly two and a half thousand years ago.
6. The ozone layer is above where weather happens. (See page 8.)
7. False. Ultra-violet light will tend to make fair-skinned people browner.
8. b) A hamburger carton might contain CFCs.

Hamburger carton

9. False. Many kinds of different plants are grown in greenhouses.
10. a) Carbon dioxide in the atmosphere acts like the glass in a greenhouse.

Greenhouse

11. a) Planting forests can help to stop global warming. Trees, and other plants, take carbon dioxide from the air to give themselves energy, in a process called photosynthesis. They give off oxygen. Forests are very important on Earth as they help to keep the correct balance of oxygen and carbon dioxide in the atmosphere.

Carbon dioxide   Oxygen

12. You would use a physical map to work out how a rise in sea level would affect the land.
13. a) and b) could cause flooding in a country.
14. c) A ham sandwich cannot be made out of plastic. Food is just about the only thing which cannot be made from plastic. Plastics can be used for almost everything else – from beach balls to aircraft fuselages.
★15. a) Recycle means "to use again".

Megaquiz answers

There are 100 possible points in the whole Megaquiz. If you score over 50 you have done well. Over **75 is excellent. You can find out more about some of the answers on the page listed after it.**

Capitals and countries

1. Canada/Ottawa.
2. New Zealand/Wellington.
3. India/Delhi.
4. Denmark/Copenhagen.
5. Argentina/Buenos Aires.
6. USA/Washington DC.
7. Australia/Canberra.
8. China/Beijing.
9. Spain/Madrid.
10. Peru/Lima.

Earth facts

1. The Pacific Ocean (page 4).
2. Antarctica (page 4).
3. b) on maps (pages 6-7).
4. a) the crust (page 5).
5. A day - 24 hours (page 3).
6. c) rivers (page 11).
7. Smaller (page 19).
8. Sea (page 12).
9. a) in the sea (page 13).
10. The Equator (page 7).

Seas and oceans

1. Atlantic Ocean (d).
2. Antarctic Ocean (f).
3. Indian Ocean (h).
4. Pacific Ocean (b).
5. Black Sea (g).
6. North Sea (e).
7. Arctic Ocean (j).
8. South China Sea (c).
9. Arabian Sea (a).
10. Mediterranean Sea (i).

People and places

1. Central Africa (page 14).
2. Japan (page 15).
3. Sahara desert (page 20).
4. Greenland (page 18).
5. Kalahari desert (page 19).
6. South American rainforest (page 20).
7. Andes (page 18).
8. China (page 15).
9. North America (page 14).
10. England (page 15).

Close-ups

1. Windmill (page 23).
2. Cocoa beans (page 21).
3. Asteroids (page 2).
4. Contour lines (page 7).
5. Tsama melons (page 19).
6. Solar panel (page 23).
7. Eskimo clothes (page 18).
8. Merino sheep (page 20).
9. Chinese rice harvester (page 15).
10. City tower block (page 16).

Countries and continents

1. Australia (e).
2. Italy (g).
3. Greece (b).
4. India (c).
5. Japan (d).
6. Canada (f).
7. Norway (h).
8. South America (i).
9. Antarctica (a).
10. Africa (j).

The sky and beyond

1. b) 1969 (page 2).
2. c) a month (page 3).
3. a) the ozone layer (page 24).
4. Mercury (page 2).
5. Hot (page 9).
6. b) a star (page 2).
7. The Universe (page 2).
8. c) plutonium (page 8).
9. Sleet.
10. A hurricane (page 9).

Misfits

1. The Moon is not a planet.
2. Tokyo is a city not a country.
3. The Mediterranean is not an ocean.
4. Lightning is not a wind.
5. Merino are sheep, not people.
6. Wood is not a fossil fuel.
7. Nuclear power is not "free" energy.
8. An axis is not a cloud.
9. Alabama is not a mountain range.
10. Nairobi is a city not a desert.

Silhouettes

1. Chopsticks (page 14).
2. Pineapple (page 21).
3. San bow and arrow (page 19).
4. Snowflake (page 8).
5. Bananas (page 21).
6. Research balloon (page 8).
7. Penguin (page 4).
8. Mbuti hut (page 19).
9. Cod (page 13).
10. Australian farm aircraft (page 20).

True or false?

1. True (page 3).
2. True (page 18).
3. False.
4. False.
5. True (page 20).
6. False.
7. False.
8. True (page 3).
9. True (page 23).
10. False.

Index

The photos on page 14 are reproduced by kind permission of the Hutchison Library.

First published in 1992 by Usborne Publishing Ltd, Usborne House, 83-85 Saffron Hill, London EC1N 8RT, England. Copyright © Usborne Publishing Ltd 1992.

The name Usborne and the device 🐝 are Trade Marks of Usborne Publishing Ltd.

AE

First published in America August 1993
Printed in Spain